I0408777

Table of Contents

Introduction

Ah, Retirement. You think you have achieved the stage of life where all your hard work finally pays off. You are looking

forward to enjoying the fruits of years of labor, saving and planning ahead. It's the time to travel, take it easy, and do the things that you put aside for the future when you have time. Ultimately, it's time for you!

But, there is just one more thing to consider before you sit back and cruise for the remainder of your life. It's time to plan for your health coverage.

Thanks to the Affordable Care Act (ACA), and the regulations found in Social Security's Program Operations Manual system (POMs) you are required to have health care coverage in order to maintain your quality of life, meet the federal guidelines and keep your Social Security benefit. During your retirement that health coverage is Medicare.

Under ACA, credible health insurance is mandated for everyone. What you may not know is that once you are retired, are at least 65 years old and are receiving Social Security benefits you **must** *accept Medicare when eligible. If you fail to accept Medicare, you will forfeit all of your Social Security benefit.*

That's right. Since 1993, you have to have health insurance, that is Medicare…or else.

So now that you know that, what do you do about it? How do you plan for it? And how do you pay for it?

When it comes to saving and investing for retirement, many Americans have done a pretty good job. The financial planners are more than willing to show us how to invest and how to save. But how many of you are planning for the mandatory expense, your health coverage? Additionally, the information is just not that easy to find.

Instead of bombarding you with 300 pages of text on the subject of Medicare, this book is a crash course on everything Medicare.

It covers:
When and Why Medicare was created. It gives you an overview of the Parts of Medicare. You will find out how to enroll, when you will be eligible and what the coverage will cost you.

We hope that this book can help you plan accordingly for the next phase of your life.

What is Medicare?

The largest health insurance program in the nation providing coverage for people that are 65 and older, and certain individuals who are under the age of 65 that have certain disabilities.

Those that qualify for Medicare, but who are under the age of 65:

Individuals that have been disabled for 24 months or longer and for those that have been diagnosed with End-Stage Renal Disease (ESRD).

When was Medicare created?

In 1965 when President Lyndon Johnson signed the Medicare and Medicaid programs into law on July 30. President Harry Truman was the first beneficiary and his wife Bess was second.

Medicaid became effective January 1, 1966, and Medicare became effective July 1, 1966.

Why was Medicare created?

The rationale behind the 1965 Medicare Act was that less than 50% of all seniors had access to health coverage in retirement, but according to the Association of American Physicians and Surgeons (AAPS) it was revealed that prior to the Medicare Act being passed, about "77% of seniors were eligible for the Kerr-Mills program (Medical Assistance for the Aged), which had been passed into law a full five years before Medicare. The remaining 23% — if they couldn't afford to pay for their own care — could receive free care at their local hospital. Under the Hill-Burton Act, hospitals agreed to provide free care to anyone who needed it in return for government grants and loans."

Who is eligible?

Eligibility for Medicare is similar to Social Security eligibility:
• Must be a US Citizen or recognized as being lawfully present in the United States.
• Those that have reached the age of 65 and have worked long enough to be eligible for Social Security or railroad retirement benefits by meeting the requirements of earning 40 credits from about 10 years of work.
• Spouses of those who have qualified.
• Government employees who may not have paid into Social Security but have paid Medicare payroll taxes while working.

What does Medicare consist of?

Medicare is broken down into different types of coverage that are recognized as letters, which are:
• Part A (Hospital Insurance)
• Part B (Medical Insurance)
• Part D (Prescription Drugs)
• Part C (Medicare Advantage Plans or private insurance)
• Supplemental Coverage - MediGap Policies

What are the costs of Medicare?

Each type of coverage has a different cost that include premiums, deductibles, co-pays and excess charges.

Please see each individual coverage for more information about each Part's premium, deductible, fee, co-pay, excess charge or other cost.

How to enroll into Medicare?

For those turning 65 and who are already receiving Social Security and/or Railroad Retiree benefits:

• You are automatically enrolled into Medicare.

• You will receive your Medicare card through the mail about 3 months prior to your 65th birthday. Keep it, and you will be enroll into Medicare Part A & B. To deny Part B coverage you will need to contact Social Security, as well as mail the card back too.

• Part A is not an option. If you are receiving Social Security, you must accept Part A or forfeit all of your current, future and even past received Social Security benefits.

For those who are not already receiving Social Security benefits, but who qualify for Medicare and who are no longer covered by credible health insurance from an employer or spouse's employer who is larger than 20 employees:

• You must enroll into Medicare during your Initial Enrollment Period (IEP), which is the 3 months prior to your 65th birthday, the month of your 65th birthday and the next 3 following months.

• If for any reason, you neglect to enroll into Medicare during your IEP and you can not prove that you have credible health coverage, Medicare may assess a late enrollment penalty on top of any Part B & D premiums you incur later on.

For those that are 65, who are not enrolled in Social Security and are currently enrolled into an employer or spouse's employer credible health plan:

• You do NOT have to enroll into Medicare until the health coverage is either given, or is no longer considered to be credible.

For those covered under an employer health plan, but the employer has 20 or fewer employees:

• The rules of the IEP stand. You must enroll into Medicare as Medicare does not recognize that size of coverage to be credible or you may be faced with late enrollment penalties for Part B & D coverage.

MediGap & Medicare Advantage Plans:

• Enrollment may commence once you are enrolled into both Medicare Part A & B.

What is Medicare Part A?

Hospital Insurance for those that have been admitted as an inpatient into a facility that is recognized by Medicare and/or the care that is provided is deemed to be medically necessary.

Who is eligible for Medicare Part A?

Those that have qualified for Medicare coverage through employment, or also through the employment of a spouse, as well as certain individuals that meet other qualifying requirements through disabilities.

What does Medicare Part A cover?

- Inpatient care received while in hospitals, skilled nursing facilities and recognized religious non-medical Health Care Institutions.

- Hospice Care for those that have less than 6 months to live and care has been prescribed by a Medicare recognized physician.

If it is has been determined that care is medically necessary and the beneficiary has been admitted to a facility as an inpatient Medicare will also cover the following:

- Anesthesia.
- Chemotherapy.
- Room and Board.
- All meals and special diets.
- General nursing.
- Medical social services.

- Physical, occupational, and speech-language therapy.
- Drugs with the exception of some self-administered drugs.
- Blood transfusions.
- Other diagnostic and therapeutic items and services.
- Medical supplies and use of equipment.
- Respite care in hospice.
- Transportation services.
- Inpatient alcohol or substance abuse treatment.
- Clinical Trials (Inpatient).
- Kidney Dialysis (Inpatient).

What does Part A not cover?

- Private duty nursing.
- Private room, unless medically necessary.
- A television or telephone in your room or personal care items like razors or slipper socks.
- Custodial care, assisted living, adult daycare, or reimbursement for family members.
- The first three pints of blood unless the blood deductible has been met.

How to enroll?

If you are already receiving Social Security benefits, you will automatically receive a red, white and blue Medicare card in the mail from Social Security.

If you are not receiving Social Security, you must enroll during the Initial Enrollment Period (IEP). This is a period of 7 months consisting of the 3 months prior to turning 65, the month of your 65th birthday and then the 3 months following your birthday.

However, if you are covered by an employer health insurance or the employer health insurance of your spouse, the IEP is the 8 months following the day of your retirement.

Please note: the start of any IEP marks the eligibility of Medicare and for those who delay enrollment they may be faced with "Late Enrollment penalties." If, however, you automatically qualify for Medicare you will not be faced with this penalty.

If you are still working and opt to take Medicare Part A, the opportunity for you to invest into a Health Savings Account (HSA) is no longer an option.

This does not mean that a person must liquidate any savings in their HSA, it only means that they can no longer contribute any new money going forward.

Medicare does not recognize COBRA as being credible health insurance coverage and retirees must enroll during their IEP or face those "Late Enrollment Penalties."

What are the costs associated to Medicare Part A?

Medicare Part A consists of many types of costs that include possible premiums, coinsurance, copays, deductibles, excess charges and other costs and they are as follows:

1) Premiums:

There are no premiums for those that have qualified for Medicare through payroll taxes from employment or a spouse's employment.

Please note that if you have not met the specific requirements of qualifying through employment you may still have an opportunity to enroll, but the premiums may be as high as $426 a month.

2) Deductibles:

There are deductibles for Medicare Part A. In 2014 the deductible for Medicare Part A is $1,216 for each annual benefit period.

3) Hospital Stays also known as coinsurance:

- Day 1-60: $0 coinsurance for each benefit period.
- Days 61-90: $304 coinsurance per day for each benefit period.
- Days 91-150: $608 coinsurance per each lifetime reserve day.
- Beyond 150 days: all costs.

Other types of coverage and costs

1) Home Health Care:

Any care that is deemed to be medically necessary that can be performed as a house call.

There is a 20% copayment for Medicare-approved durable medical equipment.

This should not be confused as Long-Term Care, as it does not provide any services to help patients with ADLs. Home Health Care only helps cover medically necessary procedures that take place in a residence.

2) Mental Health:

Medicare Part A covers mental health care services you get in a hospital if you are admitted as an inpatient. Mental health care services are available in a general hospital or a psychiatric hospital. A psychiatric hospital only cares for people with mental health conditions.

If you receive care in a psychiatric hospital (instead of a general hospital), Part A will only pay for a maximum of 190 days of inpatient psychiatric hospital services during your lifetime.

- $1,216 deductible for each benefit period
- Days 1-60: $0 coinsurance per day of each benefit period
- Days 61-90: $304 coinsurance per day of each benefit period
- Days 91-150: $608 coinsurance per each "lifetime reserve day" after day 90 for each benefit period (up to 60 days over your lifetime)
- Days 151 and beyond all costs.

20% of the Medicare-approved amount for mental health services from doctors and other providers while admitted as a hospital inpatient.

3) Skilled Nursing:

Part A will cover nursing care that is provided on a continuous, daily basis, in a skilled nursing facility. Custodial care does not qualify for Medicare Part A even if it is provided in a certified skilled nursing facility.

Examples of skilled nursing facility care include physical therapy or intravenous injections that can only be given by a registered nurse or doctor, and these costs are:

Days 1-20: $0 for each benefit period.

Days 21-100: $152 coinsurance per day of each benefit period.

Days 101 and beyond: all costs.

This is often confused with being the same as Long-Term Care coverage, but please keep in mind that this is covering just the medically necessary procedures people still need while being in a facility.

4) Hospice Care:

Care that is provided for those that have been diagnosed as terminally ill and is provided once prescribed by a Hospice Physician.

$0 for hospice care. While under Hospice all costs, with the exception of copays, are covered.

There is a copay of no more than $5 for each prescription drug and other similar products for pain relief and symptom control while at home.

There may be a 5% copay on the Medicare-approved amount for inpatient respite care.

Medicare doesn't cover room and board for hospice care in homes or any another facility that may be recognized as a residency (like a nursing home).

What is Medicare Part B?

Medicare Part B is Medical Insurance that helps pay for physician services, medical supplies, and other outpatient services that are not covered by Medicare Part A (Hospital Insurance). **This is often referred to as "Original Medicare."**

What does Part B cover?

- Doctors' services
- Outpatient hospital care
- Laboratory tests
- Outpatient physical therapy
- Certain home health care, ambulance services, medical equipment and supplies

Other services that are covered by Part B are:

- "Welcome to Medicare" visit. This is an exam that is received within the first year of enrollment
- Annual "Wellness" visits with Primary Care Physician. All costs are covered and provide a medical history, a health risk assessment, an evaluation of your physical condition, screening for cognitive impairment, including depression and it also includes a personalized prevention.

Please note that both the "Welcome to Medicare" and the Annual "Wellness" visits are NOT routine physical exams, but that they do both provide an opportunity to talk with a Primary Care Physician about any health concerns.

- Abdominal aortic aneurysm screening
- Alcohol misuse screening and counseling
- Behavioral therapy for cardiovascular disease
- Bone mass measurement
- Cardiovascular disease screenings
- Colorectal cancer screenings
- Depression screening
- Diabetes screenings
- Diabetes self-management training
- Flu shots
- Glaucoma tests
- Hepatitis B shots
- HIV screening
- Mammograms (screening)
- Obesity screening and counseling
- Pap test/pelvic exam/clinical breast exam
- Pneumococcal pneumonia shot
- Prostate cancer screening
- Sexually transmitted infection screening (STIs) and high-intensity behavioral counseling to prevent STIs
- Smoking cessation

What does Part B not cover?

Original Medicare, or Parts A & B do not cover:

- Routine Physicals
- Dental
- Vision
- Hearing
- Exams and Glasses
- Podiatry
- Cosmetic Surgery
- Acupuncture
- Care outside of the United States unless it is an emergency

Please note that if a procedure is considered to be "medically necessary" then coverage by Medicare will be allowed.

An example: *Mary had surgery to replace a detached retina that her physician prescribed as medically necessary. Not only was the procedure covered by Medicare, but her prescription glasses (one pair) were too.*

Again, as long the procedure is "medically necessary" then Medicare will cover it.

How to enroll into Medicare Part B?

Enrollment into Medicare Part B is automatic when you are eligible and if you are collecting Social Security benefits. However, if you are still working you may decline Part B until you officially retire by contacting your Medicare office.

Please keep in mind that there are premiums associated with Part B, unlike Part A, so if you are still working you may want to decline coverage until officially retired. Declining is simple as all that is needed to do is to contact the Medicare offices.

For those who are not collecting Social Security enrollment, are 65 years or older and are not covered by credible health insurance through an employer or spouse's employer, enrollment is:

Initial Enrollment Period (IEP): 7 months that include the 3 months before the 65th birthday, the month of the 65th birthday and the 3 months after.

Special Enrollment Period (SEP): the 8 months after your employment ends. Please note that Medicare does NOT recognize COBRA as credible health insurance.

And if you miss both the IEP and the SEP, meaning enrollment was delayed or missed; the next available opportunity to enroll is between January 1 and March 31st of the current year.

What is the Late Enrollment Penalty?

If you are eligible, and you miss either the IEP or the SEP, you may be required to pay a late enrollment penalty.

• The current premium plus 10% more for each 12-month cycle that coverage was delayed.

Example: *Mary retires at age 68, and chooses to accept her employer's COBRA health package for 3 years. When Mary turns 71 she discovers that Medicare does not recognize COBRA as an approved health insurance. Mary immediately enrolls in Medicare Part B, with a base premium of $104.90 for 2014. Because she did not have an approved health insurance for 3 years, Mary will pay a late enrollment penalty added to her base premium per month (3 years x (10% x $104.90) + $104.90 = $136.37).*

During 2014 the base premium plus any IRMMA plus the late enrollment penalty will automatically be deducted from any Social Security benefit she receives. The late enrollment penalty will follow her for the rest of her life.

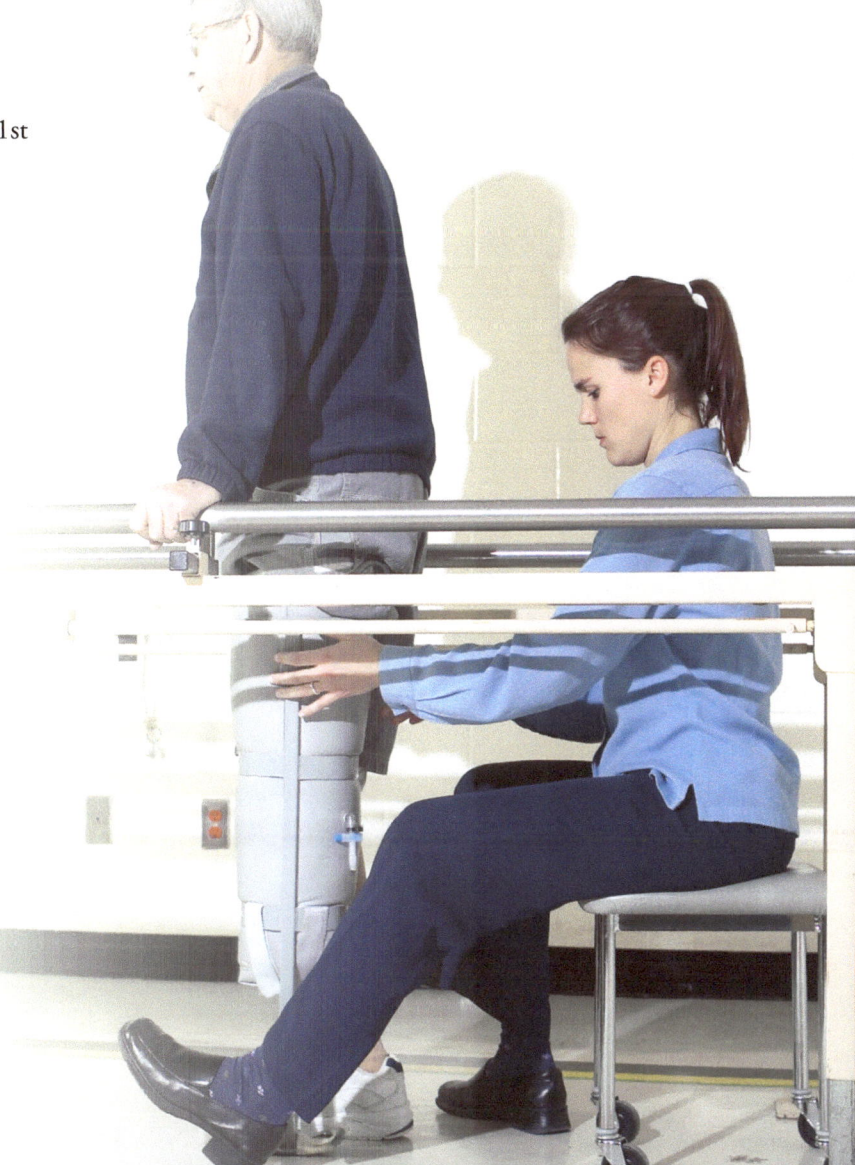

What are the costs associated to Part B?

Medicare Part B has numerous costs which are:

Premium: The standard national premium (everyone is charged the same amount unless of course someone has more money than another) in 2014 is $104.90.

As stated, Medicare, for those that have more income than others, has surcharges on top of the premium which are based on exactly how much a retiree has, which Medicare classifies as the "Income Related Monthly Adjustment Amount (IRMAA)" and this IRMAA is an extra charge added to the premium. The income amounts and penalties are as follows:

If your income in 2012 is:			
Individual	Couple	Couple File Separately	The Premium in 2014
$85,000 or less	$170,000 or less	$85,000 or less	$104.90
$85,000 - $107,000	$170,000 - $214,000	N/A	$146.90
$107,000 - $160,000	$214,000 - $320,000	N/A	$209.80
$160,000 - $214,000	$320,000 - $428,000	$85,000 - $129,000	$272.70
Greater than $214,000	Greater than $428,000	Greater than $129,000	$335.70

Please note: Medicare, when determining the surcharge, will use your tax return from the previous year, which will be the income from the year before that plus any possible income surcharge, as well as any possible late enrollment penalties, which will be deducted directly from any Social Security benefit being received.

Deductible*: $147.00 for 2014.

Coinsurance (Co-Pay)*: 20% per occurrence where specified. This coinsurance is usually part of any coverage that includes a Physician visit, Surgical Supply and or Services and Durable Medical Equipment.

Excess Charges*: The amount that the care provider is allowed by Medicare to charge on top of the total of bill.

*Indicates that these costs can be covered by certain MediGap Plans

For more information please see medicare.gov.

What are Part C Medicare Advantage Plans?

Medicare Part C is also known as Medicare Advantage Plans. This is a type of Medicare approved health plan through a private insurance company that contracts with the government to provide you with all of your Part A and Part B benefits.

Examples of Medicare Advantage Plans:

• Health Maintenance Organizations
• Preferred Provider Organizations
• Private Fee-for-Service Plans
• Special Needs Plans
• Medicare Medical Savings Account Plans

Most Medicare Advantage Plans offer Prescription Drug Coverage.

You must contract with the private insurance company for these plans, and you will not receive Medicare Part A or Part B benefits.

What do Medicare Advantage Plans offer?

These plans are required to provide all of Part A (Hospital Insurance) and Part B (Medical Insurance), and they may offer extra coverage, such as vision, hearing, dental, and/or health and wellness programs.

They are not required to cover hospice care.

Most also include Medicare prescription drug coverage (Part D), but the extra coverage is determined by the provider and the depth of the plan itself. Note that the insured are always covered for Part A and the plans must cover all of the Oservices of Medicare.

How do Medicare Advantage Plans work?

Medicare pays a fixed amount every month to the companies offering Medicare Advantage Plans in the form of subsidies.

The companies that receive these subsidies must follow rules set by Medicare, but each Medicare Advantage Plan can charge different out-of-pocket costs and have different rules for how you get services (like whether you need a referral to see a specialist or if you have to go to only doctors, facilities, or suppliers that belong to the plan for non-emergency or non-urgent care). Please note that these rules can change each year.

What are the costs associated to Medicare Advantage Plans?

Under a Medicare Advantage Plan there may be Premiums, Deductible and possibly Co-Pays. All costs are determined by the Plan Administrator and do follow Medicare guidelines.

All plan members will pay at least the Part B premium, which will be deducted directly from any Social Security benefit and with some plans, there may be another premium as well, which will be based on the type of plan selected, residency, age and health status.

Many plans may have an out-of-pocket annual maximum which is set by the companies themselves.

*The premium for Advantage Plans may be higher than the monthly premium for Medicare Part B if there is a premium.

What are the types of plans?

• **HMOs** – maintains a provider network and referrals may be necessary
• **PPOs** – also has a provider network but allows beneficiaries to obtain care outside the network if they pay higher amounts.
• **PFFS** – no network which can lead to issues finding providers that will accept it
• **SNPs** – membership is limited to certain groups of people, such as those in certain institutions (like a nursing home), those eligible for both Medicare and Medicaid, or those with certain chronic or disabling conditions.
• **HMOPOS** – an HMO plan that may let you get some services out of network for a higher cost.
• **MSA** – Medical Savings Accounts

Do Medicare Advantage Plans cover Prescription Drug Coverage?

Yes and there are two options that a beneficiary may take:

1. If a beneficiary opts to select a PPO or an HMO plan then the beneficiary must enroll in the provided Rx plan.

2. If a beneficiary decides to elect a PFFS plan then the beneficiary may choose either the plan's Rx coverage, if offered, or a stand-alone Drug Plan.

Is there anything else that needs to be known about Medicare Advantage Plans?

Even though a beneficiary may choose a Medicare Advantage Plan, they are still subject to Medicare's income limitations, and any surcharge will be automatically deducted from any Social Security benefit.

It is illegal for someone to sell a person a MediGap Policy if there is already an Advantage Plan in effect.

What are the advantages and disadvantages to a Medicare Advantage Plan?

(This is not an endorsement of any one plan or company nor is it an endorsement of Advantage Plans over "Original Medicare" or vice versa).

The Pros to Advantage Plans

Random Insurance Companies PPO;

- The possibility to choose any doctor or hospital, and if services are received from in-network providers then costs may be lower, even when traveling.
- Affordable monthly plan premium for most plans may be available.
- Referral-free visits to any provider nationwide.
- The ability to create prescription drug coverage that may be equal to or better than the standard requirement for a Medicare Part D plan.
- Possible emergency coverage anywhere in the world.
- Affordable co-payments for doctor visits and annual routine physicals if the plan permits.

- Coverage for annual screenings at no charge.
- Out-of-pockets costs that may be lower especially if an in-network provider is selected.
- All the benefits of "Original Medicare" and the opportunity to create more, including:
- Prescription drug coverage (some plans do not include drug coverage).
- Emergency coverage when you travel outside the United States.
- The option to also have a plan that will cover Dental, Vision, Hearing, Wellness/Fitness Benefits and Podiatry.

The Cons to an Advantage Plan:

From a report created by the Medicare Rights Center that is based on thousands of beneficiary calls to the Medicare Rights Center, it lists nine common problems with Medicare Advantage plans that include the following:

- Care can cost more than it would under "Original Medicare."
- Private plans are not stable and may suddenly cease coverage.
- Members may experience difficulty getting emergency or urgent care.
- Because plans only cover certain doctors, the continuity of care is often broken when the plan drops a health care provider.
- Members have to follow plan rules to get covered care.
- Members are restricted in their choices of doctors, hospitals, and other providers.
- It can be difficult to get care away from home (i.e., Traveling).
- The extra benefits offered often turn out to be less than promised.

For more information:
Medicare.gov
Medicarerights.org
Elder Law Answers.com

What is Medicare Part D?

A federal program that is part of Medicare that helps subsidize the cost of medications for those enrolled in the program.

Each plan is administered by a private health insurance company that is overseen by the Centers of Medicare and Medicaid Systems (CMS).

When did Part D become part of Medicare?

Part D was created in 2006 with the passing of the Medicare Prescription Drug, Improvement, and Modernization Act of 2003 (MMA).

At the time of passing of the MMA in 2003, the costs for medications were either covered by Medicare Parts A & B, through prescriptions written by physicians after an admitted medical necessary inpatient visit to a hospital/caregiver or directly by the Medicare beneficiary, as they were fully responsible for funding 100% of the costs of any medications needed.

The problem, obviously, was the fact that those seniors who needed medications to continue daily living standards, but that did not need to be admitted into a hospital, were put into the position to have to fund for their medications themselves.

Part D was designed to help seniors who fell into this predicament with being able to purchase a type of health insurance that would offset the cost of medications. Today there are 2 ways to receive the much needed health insurance to cover medications in retirement:

1. Stand alone policy, which is purchased through a private insurance company in conjunction with "Original Medicare."

2. Purchased along side, or within a Medicare Advantage Plan.

What does Part D cover?

Each plan must cover a standard level of medications which is set by Medicare each year, unfortunately, this list can change and has for the most part changed annually.

With each Part D policy, either through a standalone policy in conjunction with "Original Medicare" or one that is attached to a Medicare Advantage plan, there is a list of medications that each plan will cover which is better known, as a formulary.

Every health plan that is covering medications provides a list giving details of medicines that Medicare Part D will cover for the contract term, along with all of the costs associated with the plan.

This list or formulary is broken down into what is referred to as Tiers.

These Tiers range from 1 to 4, are designed to detail the over-all costs associated with the drugs that are covered.

Currently, these 4 Tiers are ranked from the cheapest to the most expensive, and they are:

1. Tier 1 - Generic Drugs.
2. Tier 2 - Some Brand Name Drugs and some Generic Drugs.
3. Tier 3 - All Brand Name Drugs.
4. Tier 4 - Drugs chosen by the Insurance Companies to be not subject to any of the rules & regulations set forth by Medicare.
   a. There are two subset Tiers in this category:
      i. "Injectable" medications.
      ii. "Living organism" medications.

Please note that health insurance providers may have coverage rules for each "Tier", meaning that a beneficiary may have to adhere to certain procedures or meet some form of requirements before the health insurance provider will cover a certain drug.

These rules may include:

- **"Step Therapy"** authorization, this where a beneficiary must first be prescribed a like medication that is on a lower Tier before receiving a higher cost/higher Tier medication.
- **"Prior Authorization"**, meaning that the physician must, before being prescribing the medication, contact the health insurance provider and show that there is a medically necessary need for that specific medication.

What are the costs of Part D?

The costs per plan will vary by the rates set forth by the Private Insurers who administer the coverage and can be based on residency, gender, health and income. An example of what may be charged is as follows:

- A monthly premium – according to Q1Medicare.com, the national average monthly premium was $53.26.
- A yearly deductible ($310 for the standard plan in 2014).
- Co-payments or coinsurance (25% for Tier 1-3 medications: 33% to 35% for Tier 4 medications).

To find out which plan may be best please see Medicare's Plan Finder at:

https://www.medicare.gov/find-a-plan/questions/home.aspx

For the **late enrollment penalty** in 2014, the Part D base beneficiary premium for 2014 is $32.42; this is the amount that is used to determine the late enrollment penalty associated with Part D coverage.

As stated, Medicare Part is also ruled under the Income Related Monthly Adjustment Amount (IRMAA) which is an extra charge added to the premium due to having "too much" income in retirement. The income amounts and penalties are as follows:

If your income in 2012 is:			
Individual	Couple	Couple File Separately	The Premium in 2014
$85,000 or less	$170,000 or less	$85,000 or less	Premium
$85,000 - $107,000	$170,000 - $214,000	N/A	Premium + $12.10
$107,000 - $160,000	$214,000 - $320,000	N/A	Premium + $31.10
$160,000 - $214,000	$320,000 - $428,000	$85,000 - $129,000	Premium + $50.20
Greater than $214,000	Greater than $428,000	Greater than $129,000	Premium + $69.30

Who is eligible for Part D coverage?

- Anyone already enrolled into Medicare Parts A & B
- You must live in the plan's service area (you cannot have a plan from a different state).
- Those that live outside of the US & territories and those who are incarcerated are NOT eligible.

When is enrollment to join Part D?

Initial Enrollment Period (IEP):

- 3 months before 65th Birthday, the month of the 65th Birthday and then the next 3 months after or
- 8-month period following the retirement of an employer at or past the age of 65.

Annual Enrollment Period (AEP):

- Oct 15 thru Dec 7 (Changes are effective Jan 1). This period is for anyone who did not enroll into a plan during their IEP when first eligible due to retirement.

Dis-enrollment Period:

The opportunity to cancel a Medicare Advantage Plan and switch back to "Original Medicare," this allows the retiree the ability to purchase a stand alone Drug Plan (Part D):

- Jan 1 thru Feb 14

Special Enrollment Periods:

Any period where a person may enroll into a Medicare Plan that is not the IEP or the AEP:

- If someone moves from State to another. In order to qualify for Medicare Part D coverage as well as a MediGap policy you must reside, permanently, in the State where the plans where purchased.
- If one was to lose other credible drug coverage (meaning a plan was canceled by the provider).
- Enter or leave a Long Term Care facility.
- Qualify for extra help / lose qualification for extra help – meaning the ability to afford certain types of coverage has changed.
- 5 Star Plans – A person can enroll one time only at any point per year in any plan that is ranked by CMS as a 5 star.

Late Enrollment Penalty;

Impacts only those that delayed their enrollment into Medicare and who did NOT have credible health coverage.

The penalties can be expected to be:

• 1% of the National Base Premium added to their Part D premium for each month missed (in 2014 the base premium is $32.42).

An example: *Mary retires at age 68 and chooses to enroll into her employer's COBRA health package for her health insurance needs instead of Medicare, as she feels the coverage is better.*

By the time Mary reaches the age of 71 she realizes that Medicare, unfortunately, does not recognize COBRA as credible health insurance and enrolls immediately into a Prescription Drug, Part D Plan which has a premium of $75 a month.

Because of her delay in enrolling into Medicare, even though she did have COBRA health insurance, she is considered to be a late enroller into Medicare for the past 3 years or 36 months.

The penalty for this delay will result in an increase of her current Medicare Part D premium for the year or $11.70 a month (1% x $32.42 x 36) which will be added to her premium making her total costs for her Part D coverage total $86.70 a month.

Please note that the surcharges for the late enrollment penalty are automatically deducted from any Social Security benefit received and that each late enrollment penalty will follow you for the remainder of your retirement - that 36% penalty Mary has will be added on to whatever her premium will be for the remainder or her life.

For more information see www.medicare.gov

What are MediGap Plans?

MediGap Plans, which are commonly referred to as a form of "Supplemental" Coverage are health policies that are administered by Private Insurance Companies to be used in-conjunction with "Original Medicare" to cover the "Gaps" that are in "Original Medicare."

Every plan, which is regulated by Medicare, is the same across the country, with exceptions only in 3 states (MA, WI, MN) where the only difference is the cost and the rate of inflation at which a plan may grow.

So a MediGap Plan A policy will be exactly the same, in terms of what is covered, in Arkansas as it is in Rhode Island. The only difference may be the costs and how the premiums each year are calculated.

What are those gaps?

The gaps consist of both lack of coverage and also expenses or charges. For example, under "Original Medicare" a hospital stay is really only covered 100% for 60 days, with a certain type of MediGap Plan the coverage would be extended for a full year.

As for the expenses: certain MediGap Plans can cover all the co-pays, deductibles and any excess charges that are a part of Medicare Part A and or B.

These gaps are as follows:

Coverage for Blood: Medicare only covers the first 3 pints of blood, which in most hospitalizations without "bleeding or lacerations" should be sufficient. For those needing emergency care from an accident or wound, more than 3 pints may be needed.

Hospital stays: Medicare covers the first 60 days of any stay in a hospital due to any one incident after the current year's deductible.

- Between days 61 – 90 there is a co-pay of $283 per day per stay while Medicare covers all other costs.
- 91-150, the co-insurance is $566 per day per stay; Medicare picks up the rest.
- All costs for each day beyond 150 days are covered by the beneficiary.

Co-pays & Deductibles: As stated above, Part A & Part B both have a deductible that can be covered by certain types of MediGap Plans.

Foreign Travel: "Original Medicare" will not cover any health costs while incurred out of the country, with a proper Gap Plan emergency care can be covered.

For most beneficiaries on Medicare, there are 10 Plans (A-N with nothing for E & I) to choose from and each have certain aspects that they cover or don't cover. These three states, Massachusetts, Minnesota, and Wisconsin have a different set up.

Examples of the Plans:

Plan A; the most basic and the building block of all other Plans, covers an additional 365 days of hospitalization, any coinsurance (not except on skilled nursing) and Blood.

Plan F; (the most robust) covers everything in Plan A and all deductibles, excess charges & foreign travel emergency care.

*Some of the 10 standard plans pay for services not covered by Medicare such as outpatient prescription drugs, preventive screening, and emergency medical care while traveling outside the United States. Coverage is also provided in some plans for health care provider charges in excess of Medicare's approved amount and for some care in your home, but these are all based on the Plan chosen.

Unfortunately, Medicare also has many other "Gaps" that are not covered, such as coverage for Dental, Vision, Hearing and Podiatry. In order to insure against these possible costs a beneficiary needs to look into a Medicare Advantage Plan.

Please note that it is against the rules to own both a MediGap Plan and a Medicare Advantage Plan.

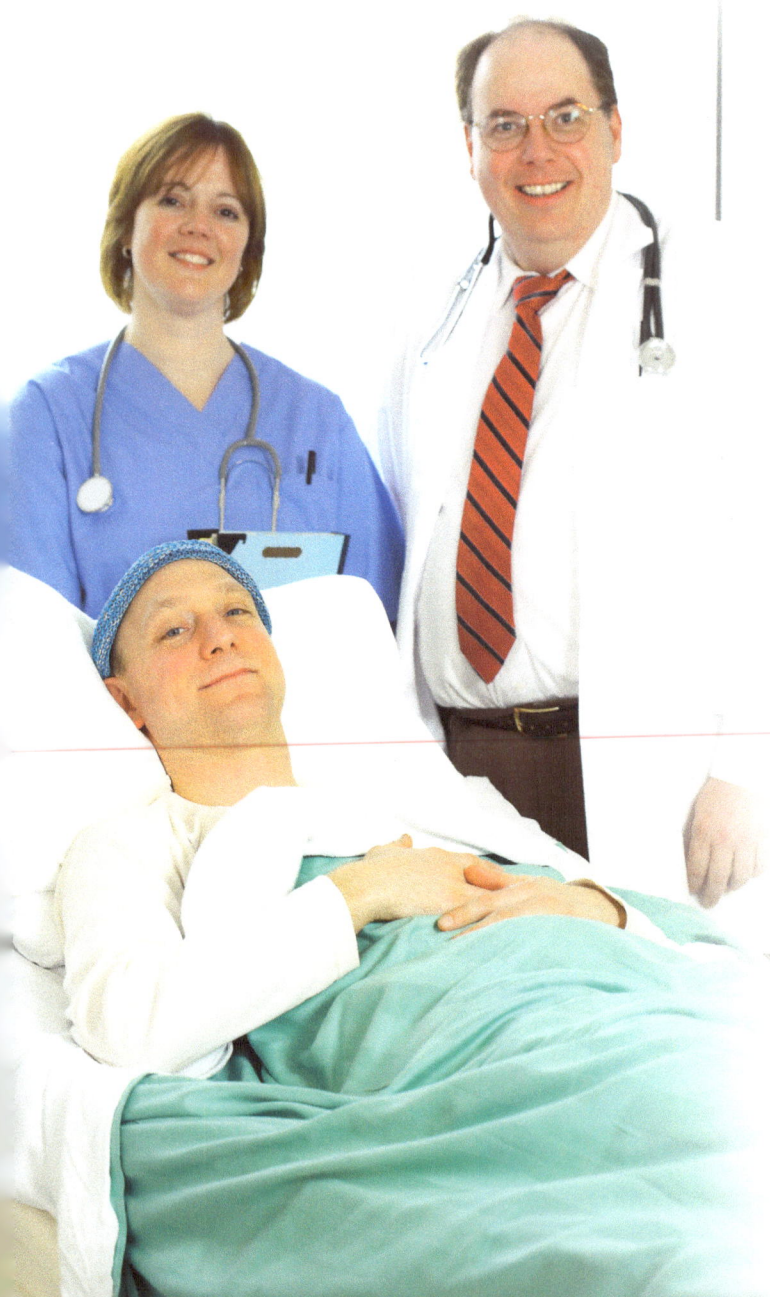

What are the costs associated with a MediGap Plan?

Premiums: They will be determined by the private insurance provider that is administering the plan and even though benefits are identical for all MediGap plans, premiums vary from one company to another and then depending on what area too.

There are 3 ways to calculate premiums:

1. Issue Age: If the plan is purchased at age 65, you will always pay the same premium the company charges people who are 65 regardless of your age.

2. Attained Age: The premium is based on your current age and will increase as you mature. Under this type of plan the cost of a Gap Plan for 75-year old person will be much more expensive than a plan for a 65-year old person.

3. No Age: Everyone pays the same premium regardless of age, and the state must approve the rates.

How to Enroll into a MediGap Plan:

MediGap Plans are available to anyone who is enrolled into "Original Medicare" which includes Part B. For those who enroll into Part B during their Initial Enrollment Period (IEP) or their Special Enrollment Period (SEP) they have a 6 month guaranteed issue opportunity. This means that the company cannot deny or condition the issuance or effectiveness, or discriminate in the pricing of a policy because of medical history, health status or claims experience. All have to be accepted.

Keep in mind that after both the IEP & the SEP the private insurer that is administering the MediGap Plan can impose the preexisting condition restrictions, charge more for coverage, or flat out reject any applicant based on health conditions. Also, after the IEP or SEP, the only time that a person can purchase a MediGap Plan is during open enrollment which is October 15 to December 7 of any year. The effective date of the policy will begin January 1 of the next year.

Please note that a change of residency, from one state to another, will trigger the Special Enrollment Period and a person can enroll into any MediGap Plan that they so choose at any period, but they will still be subject to the terms and conditions of the private health insurer.

MediGap Plans Breakdown:

Benefits	A	B	C	D	E	F	G	H	I	J	K	L	M	N
Part A Coinsurance & Hospital Costs up to an additional 365 days.	✔	✔	✔	✔	✔	✔	✔	✔	✔	✔	✔	✔	✔	✔
Part B Co-Pay for other than Preventive Services	✔	✔	✔	✔	✔	✔	✔	✔	✔	✔	50%	75%	✔	✔***
Blood (First 3 Pints)	✔	✔	✔	✔	✔	✔	✔	✔	✔	✔	50%	75%	✔	✔
Part A Hospice Care Co-Pay	✔	✔	✔	✔		✔	✔				50%	75%	✔	✔
Skilled Nursing Facility Care Co-Pay		✔	✔	✔	✔	✔	✔	✔	✔	✔	50%	75%	✔	✔
Part A Deductible		✔	✔	✔	✔	✔	✔	✔	✔	✔	50%	75%	50%	
Part B Deductible			✔			✔				✔				
Part B Excess Charges						✔		✔	✔					
Foreign Travel Emergency (up to plan limits)		✔	✔	✔	✔	✔	✔	✔	✔	✔			✔	✔
Part B Preventive Care Co-Pay	✔	✔	✔	✔	✔	✔	✔	✔	✔	✔	✔	✔	✔	✔

Plan F offers a high deductible plan. If you choose this option, this means you must pay for Medicare covered costs up to the deductible amount of $2,140 in 2014 before your MediGap Plan pays anything.

**After meeting the out-of-pocket yearly limit & your yearly Part B deductible, the MediGap Plan pays 100% of covered services for the rest of the calendar year.*

*** Plan N pays 100% of the Part B Coinsurance, except for a co-payment of up to $20.00 for some office visits and up to a $50.00 co-payment for emergency room visits that do NOT result in inpatient admission.*

If you live in Massachusetts, Minnesota or Wisconsin MediGap Policies have a different set of standards.

Dan McGrath

Mr. McGrath is considered to be one of the nation's leading experts on the subject of how health related costs will affect retirement, the financial planning process as well as the overall economy.

He is the Co-Founder of Jester Financial Technologies, a firm dedicated to providing the key education and software tools for financial advisors and investors to use in order to determine the expected costs for health coverage in retirement. Jester Financial has recently been chosen to provide the health care data for Money Guide Pro, the country's leading financial planning software, which is currently utilized in over 90 different financial firms and financial industry organizations.

Mr. McGrath has also authored the bestselling retirement planning book *What You Don't Know About Retirement Will Hurt You* as well as authoring numerous articles and whitepapers on the subjects of Health Costs, Medicare, Social Security, the Affordable Care Act and Retirement Planning.

He has also co-authored a module for the Retirement Income Industry Association's (RIIA) *A View Across the Silos*, has been a guest Medicare specialist for Horsesmouth's *Savvy Medicare Planning for Baby Boomers* as well as hosting BISK's CPEasy platform for Certified Public Accountants and has written the Medicare content for some of the leading financial firms in the country.

He can be heard as a radio personality on WSMN 1590 AM, Nashua New Hampshire's Source for News and Talk Radio, as he hosts Eyes and Ears Wide Open, along with being a reoccurring guest on America Tonight with Kate Delaney.

www.ingramcontent.com/pod-product-compliance
Lightning Source LLC
Chambersburg PA
CBHW060826290526
45792CB00005BB/1818